A LIFE WORTH LIVING

A LIFE WORTH LIVING

DIANE SWAFFIELD

The Elonias Foundation

Copyright © 2023 by The Elonias Foundation

All rights reserved. No part of this book may be reproduced in any manner whatsoever without written permission except in the case of brief quotations embodied in critical articles and reviews.

First Printing, 2020. This edition, 2023.
ISBN: 978-1-7385803-2-3

Foreword

by Jason Swaffield

In loving memory of my Diane ...

Diane was the example of what is possible. How else does one share words about someone who was the truest representation of the light of awareness I have ever known? Someone who was an inspiration. A warrior. An investigator and a mentor. Diane was a beautiful person. Loving, giving and kind with a joyous laugh that matched a fabulous sense of humour. A quick wit. As smart as they come. Always challenging the status quo to find the truth. And that is where the definition of who Diane was, really begins.

As her husband, I understand people may expect me to say such things about the woman I loved, and still love. I can understand that. However, for 20 years Diane and I shared everything - our 'outer' and our true 'inner'. We shared a deeply meaningful life of purpose and profound discoveries through our need to investigate life and the realms beyond it.

Diane was in life, and still is beyond it, an extraordinary person and 'being'. Anyone who knew Diane would surely agree.

So how does one write in an introduction to a book so personal, so vast and so important? You do what that person would have done. You speak from your heart. As Diane would often say, "You have to tell a story from the beginning." This is no ordinary story, however, as Diane was no ordinary person.

I am writing this foreword to Diane's book 'A Life Worth Living' because my beautiful wife passed over from this life, this reality, in early 2020. 'A Life Worth Living' tells only the start of her story of over 40 years of extraordinary investigation. It is a testament to her dedication, her tireless energy and burning desire to discover the very meaning of all life everywhere. Diane's determination to understand the purpose behind it all was her mission, equaled only by her compassion and love for the Great Beings who walked beside her in her life, and beyond it, on her 'Journey Home'.

This is why 'A Life Worth Living' is a part of Diane's journey home. It is a message for anyone who feels a 'stirring within'. A recognition there is more to discover. More to remember. Diane spent the greater part of her life investigating the purpose of 'life' - the afterlife, deeper levels of consciousness, reality itself, illusion, the paranormal and 'time' just to name a few.

I am humbled, enlightened and 'I remember' because of it. There is far more to life, to each of us, and to reality itself than we realise. It is time to wake up!

Diane began to write this book as a continuation of her life's work, and although it will never have an ending on paper, as such, it will live on in her name so others can hopefully find theirs, and be free from illusion entirely.

Diane wanted to share the story of her extraordinary life with you so her experiences could give insight, inspiration and courage to look further, dig deeper, and ask questions. To be true to what resonates inside 'you'. To have the courage to believe we are more than 'who' we think we are, and remember 'what' we really are. To ask questions. To have the freedom to find answers. Because life is not what we are told to believe it is. Not at all.

Diane writes as she lived, with honesty and integrity. Always exploring, always personal. With a dedication to finding the truth no matter where it may lead. Diane's life was a journey of experiences, embracing change and overcoming great challenges.

Diane did not live an easy life. She chose to keep moving beyond the sameness and to ignore the obstacles and illusion of fear that keep so many bound to their beliefs. Diane journeyed beyond the boundaries of belief, again and again.

Diane found answers by never giving up, and nor should any one who seeks to remember. To give up is to allow the sameness of life to decide your fate. No way! We all have to be willing to let go of beliefs in order to grow and remember a greater part of ourselves, and why we are here. There is so much to remember.

Diane walked her pathway with strength, grace and humility. She kept moving on her journey - no matter what. That, I believe, is one of the most important virtues we can learn from Diane in order for each and every one of us to find our way to happiness and 'home'.

So how do you write something for many to read that shares the totality of knowing someone so special, so extraordinary?

You have to write it, and trust others read it, with their 'inner sound'. That is the only way to share an insight into the light of awareness that was Diane. And after all, light is love.

How do you encapsulate love? You do it with love. How do you introduce a 'A Life Worth Living' and try to give meaning to words that will forever fall short of the Real thing?

You don't. You let that person speak for themselves. I hope you enjoy reading Diane's 5th book, 'A Life Worth Living'.

In loving memory,
Jason

A Life Worth Living

A good story comes from your heart and not your head. It should be told as if it was being re-lived all over again, with each memory powerfully expressing itself in the most truthful way. This includes the memories you want to remember, as well as the memories you would sooner forget. That is how I will share my story, my life, which I have given the most apt title – "A Life Worth Living".

I realise that it will take considerable courage and tenacity to delve deeply into the recesses of memory, where pain and despair reside. How easy it would be to skim the surface and present what is acceptable, rather than what is confronting. However, to do so would defeat the purpose and the reason behind this story being told.

Why do I have the need to tell the story of my life? The answer is very simple. I want others to know that life is not what it appears to be, for there is so much more. In knowing that, then there is a choice. The choice to remember or to forget.

It all depends upon whether you want to have a life that is chosen for you, or to live a life that you choose to have. My life has been a roller coaster ride of discovery and regret. It is within the discovery that you find your real true self. Regret, however, takes you on a journey of self- indulgence that leads nowhere. Always believing you are the victim and you are powerless to change it.

If you stay too long in regret, you become totally lost, and memory becomes your master. It has a way of amplifying what went wrong, rather than what could have gone right. It's all a matter of perspective.

Behind every person's life, there is a story to tell. Autobiographies and biographies of the famous and the rich have always been well sought after. From adventurers, celebrities, heroes, sporting identities and even criminals, the shelves in the book shops are full. So why would my life story even rate a mention? I'm not famous, and certainly not rich. What I can state however, is that I have lived a life that is so very different from anyone else I know, and I need to tell the story before the storyteller has completed the story.

If you are willing to go the distance and follow me to the end, then I say thank you. If you are open to the possibility that what I have to tell you is true, then I can't ask for anything more. It happened, it really happened, and to deny it would be to deny my life, and I can't do that.

Chapter 1

I cannot count the years before I reached 28 as being important to this story, except to say that my childhood and young adult years were all about change. Being born in England and coming to Australia at the tender age of 9 helped me to develop an independent and outgoing nature. My mother went to work for the first time since before I was born, and I had to grow up really fast – and I did.

What I remember most about that time was coming home from school to an empty house. In England, not only was my mother home, but my grandmother also lived with us. The empty house that was so cold in winter was not what I was used to. However, it helped me establish my independence at an early age, and looking back now, I can see why.

Deep inside everyone's psyche there is a special place where hopes and dreams live. Sometimes they surface and are acted upon, but more often than not they are relegated to our daydreams and wish list. We are careful not to share them with strangers, but often speak about them to the special people in our lives. Hopes and dreams help us in our darker times when something happens in our life that is difficult to bear. Without them, we would feel so alone and so afraid.

As long as I can remember, I have been interested in what I couldn't see, and ghost stories especially, held me captive for hours. I remember a time when I was at school, during library class, I found a book on ghosts and was so engrossed in it, that I didn't hear the bell or even the sound of my class mates leaving the room. It wasn't until the teacher came right up to my desk and asked me if I was going to sit there all day, did I realise I was the only one left in the room.

My special place has always held my dream to know what life really means. From a very early age I have asked the unanswerable age-old questions "Where was I before I was born? Where do I go when I die? and What is the purpose to my life?" Not only were my parents unable to answer these questions, I just couldn't find anyone who could. However, deep inside myself, I truly believed that one day I would find out. This story is all about my journey towards finding the answer.

I have discovered that there is a purpose to all life, involving a synchronicity that links everything together. All has a special part to play, and all belongs together as one. Individuality is simply an expression of life, enabling the "one" of itself to experience so many variables, and whilst we are so entrenched in handed-down structured beliefs, we cannot understand the true nature of ourselves.

Unfortunately it is commonplace to follow a pathway set for us to follow in the tradition of what others have done before us. Many follow blindly the beliefs that have been handed down from one generation to the next. Going against the majority is never easy, but it is often the few that make the difference.

Beliefs are like stone blocks, they are so difficult to move, for they form the backbone and foundation of our society. History has recorded that too many people are prepared to kill and even die to protect what they believe in.

Our society and the world in which we live is fashioned upon beliefs. There are harsh penalties for those who do not abide by the beliefs they have to have. Religion and culture have been formed upon beliefs, and woe betide anyone who comes along and says that they are wrong! It is all about power and control, and the real true nature of what life really means is hidden under the tyranny of the ruling few.

Against this backdrop, my story begins. At 28 years of age the answers to the questions that I had began to surface. When the timing is right, then the door opens. My door opened up to reveal a well known medium from England by the name of Doris Stokes, who had the ability to speak to the "dead".

Imagine my delight, when prime-time TV embraced her. Her audiences were enthralled with messages from beyond the grave, as so was I. Here was someone who could actually talk to the dead! She was a humble and caring woman who captured everyone's hearts with her sensitivity towards the families who were still grieving for what they believed they had lost.

It was Doris Stokes who was the catalyst in changing my life forever, and through a work colleague of my mother's who attended the Spiritualist Church, I took the opportunity to learn so much more.

The first time I went to a Spiritualist Church service I was amazed by the fact that the sermon appeared to be sending everyone to sleep! Nearly everyone was sitting there with their eyes closed, and I remember feeling somewhat amused at the time by what I was observing. Little did I realise at the time that they were simply closing their eyes to their surroundings in order to listen more deeply to what was being said.

I found the service interesting, but it wasn't what you would call enthralling, and I was beginning to think that perhaps I had made a mistake in coming. It wasn't until a young woman was introduced as someone who was going to give "proof of survival", that I really sat up and took notice. This is what I had come for. What if she chose me?

She certainly wasn't a Doris Stokes, but the messages she gave, supposedly from friends and family who had died, seemed to make people happy and sometimes even a little emotional. I was hooked! I didn't get a message that night, but it was enough to make me want to come back again. That was the beginning of my roller coaster ride into the paranormal.

I went back to the Church every Sunday evening. Many of the lectures in the service were complex, and even though I tried really hard to follow what they were talking about, I inadvertently lost the plot. It was time to find out how I could learn more.

The Church ran a development group to train people to develop insight and intuition. These groups were invitation only" as places were limited and well sought after and there was usually a waiting period before you are invited to attend.

So, imagine my excitement, when only after attending the church for several weeks, I was approached by the Minister of the Church and asked if I would like to join their development group. I didn't need to be asked twice. It was everything that I had wanted, and I just couldn't wait to begin. It was held in a renovated garage that was used on Sundays for the Church service, and I remember the first time I went there.

There were approximately 20 chairs placed in a circle, and the room was dimly lit by a red light. Sitting down, I felt both excited and nervous. Little did I realise, what was about to happen next would change my life forever.

We were all instructed to close our eyes and relax. I remember wishing there was music playing, but instead there was only silence. Closing my eyes I attempted to still my thoughts, but it wasn't easy. I don't know how long had passed, when I heard someone breathing deeply, as if they had fallen into a deep sleep. It sounded close by. My curiosity got the better of me, so I decided to take a peek.

That was when things got really serious! My eyes wouldn't open, and I couldn't move. I felt terrified!

It was then that I heard a voice. It was the lady conducting the group. Thank goodness she had seen my predicament. She was telling me everything was alright. She might have thought so, but I certainly didn't! Then it suddenly dawned on me - the sound of the deep breathing that I had heard earlier, it was coming from me!

I just couldn't move at all. My eyes seemed glued shut and my arms and legs refused to budge. This was no joke, and I was really scared. Then suddenly, it was all over. I was able to open my eyes and move my body. I looked up to find her standing in front of me, smiling as if I had achieved some sort of admirable feat. "Close your eyes" she said. "Everything is alright".

At that point, you either give up or you go on, and I wasn't about to give up. So, wrestling with my courage, I closed my eyes again. This time I felt myself moving backwards very quickly.

I would describe it as going down a long tunnel you can't see. I could feel the chair beneath me, but felt I was somewhere else at the same time. It was really weird, but this time I felt much calmer.

In order to describe what happened next, I will have to be as descriptive as I can, because it was the turning point of my life ...

As I said before, I felt in a dual state of consciousness, existing in two places at once, aware of the room I was in, but also being aware of existing away from myself. I then heard myself speaking, but I didn't have any control over what I was saying. The words somehow being formed independently from my own thoughts. That's the crazy part of it all. Whilst you are thinking one thing, you are speaking about something else. I heard myself talking, and yet it wasn't me!

Then it just stopped. I found myself back in the chair, totally aware of my surroundings and the duality of consciousness had completely disappeared. I sat there in total shock, not quite knowing what to think. When the group ended, the lady sitting next to me said in a very envious tone "I have been coming here for years, and I don't get anything. This is your first time, and look what happened to you!"

I certainly didn't want it to ever happen again. My idea of intuitive development was to be able to see what the future held. Not to have something or someone affect your body in such a manner. I decided then and there that I wouldn't be coming back. No way. How naive and idealistic I was. You just don't get on the train and expect to get off. It's that simple. The train left the station that night on a journey that was to last a lifetime.

From that night onwards, my intuitive ability just expanded. I always believed I had good insight into things, but had never thought of myself as psychic. So did I go back? Oh yes, I did. Something had happened - but what?

I needed to know, and so my quest for answers began.

That was 28 years ago.

Chapter 2

When you touch something outside of your understanding, even outside your concept of what reality is, you begin to experience a heightened sense of uncertainty. Your world has suddenly changed. There is something you cannot see and something you cannot hear, but it seems to know all about you.

You find yourself switching between excitement in the day and fear during the night. It's amazing how brave you feel when the sun is shining and people are going about their daily business. However, when the sun goes down and it becomes quiet and dark, then you find yourself looking over your shoulder, and every unknown noise startles you.

One night, only a few weeks after my experience at the development group, I decided to get up the courage and challenge who or whatever it was. At the time I was suffering from very bad headaches due to blocked sinuses, and I felt pretty miserable. Lying in bed and gathering all my courage, I mentally sent out a challenge. "Whoever you are, prove to me that you can hear me. I need you to fix my headaches".

How pompous and arrogant can you get? At the time I didn't think so, but looking back now, I shudder at how I sounded. Well, I didn't have long to wait. I didn't really expect anything to happen, but it did.

Someone or something had taken hold of my nose and was tightly pinching it! The shock of it all sent me immediately under the covers, wishing I hadn't said anything at all. Of course, that didn't work and my nose was still being squeezed. What happened next was amazing. Imagine something you can't see tightly holding your nose. You just feel panic. Then why don't I remember anything else until the morning? It sounds strange, but I had gone to sleep.

On that day and the next, my nose just ran. It was obvious that my sinuses had been unblocked, and I didn't have another sinus headache for years after that. Needless to say, I was very thankful, but was reluctant to send out a challenge again.

Every Wednesday night was group night, and I looked forward to it all week. One night we were given homework to do through the week. We were asked to sit quietly with pen and paper and do what is called "inspirational writing". Never having done that before, I hoped that I wouldn't end up with a blank sheet. Well, there I was, propped up in my bed. The children were asleep and my husband was watching television. I finally had some free time.

I held the pen in my hand and waited. Ten minutes went by, and nothing. Perhaps I was doing something wrong. Then I realised that I was waiting, rather than listening. I closed my eyes and did just that. I listened. My head became light and a warm feeling came over me. I felt the familiar feeling of being disconnected from myself.

Opening my eyes, I began to write. Just a few words at a time came into my mind. I didn't know or even think about what the next words would be. Just as I finished writing the words that were in my mind, a few more words came to me, and so it went. Four pages later it all stopped.

I felt an overwhelming rush of emotion, and then it was gone. Whatever had happened showed itself in the complexity of what was written. Instead of having some inspirational message about friendship or love, it was all about time and space. A subject that I knew nothing about, or even had an interest in at the time.

The object of the exercise was to be impressed with inspiration from the spiritual worlds. I would have been happy to have received words to inspire the living from those who had gone beyond the veil of death, and who were so much wiser for the experience. But time and space .. what was that all about?

I am ashamed to say that I didn't take what I had written to the group. Somehow it just didn't fit in. As expected, others came with what they had written. Words of love, hope and encouragement to live life to its fullest. Just what I had hoped to receive. When asked where mine was, I just simply shrugged my shoulders and told them that I wasn't able to get anything. What a fool I was then. The most powerful experience is often overlooked when your expectations run in a different direction.

If I could turn back the clock now, I would have proudly shared what I was given, and I wouldn't have cared what anyone thought.

What I wrote that night was profound, and it was the first of so much more that I would write over the years. My interest in the paranormal grew. I found myself becoming more and more obsessed with the need to know what was behind it all, and what did it all mean. Life seemed so incidental and mundane in comparison. I read every book I could get my hands on that spoke about life after death. If I couldn't go to the Spiritualist Church on Sundays because of family commitments, I felt empty inside. I was hooked!

At 30 years of age, I had two children. A daughter who was 5, and a son who was 3 years of age. One night my daughter woke me up, to tell me that she had wet her bed. Something that she hadn't done since she was a baby. Half asleep, I went to the cupboard to fetch clean sheets. As I was re-making her bed, I felt a click in my back. There was no pain involved. Instead I felt a rush of heat travel up my body, and in it's wake, I felt extremely unwell. Quickly putting her back to bed, I made my way to the toilet.

Looking back now, I don't know why I didn't go back to bed. However, at the time, the toilet seemed the best place to be. I remember feeling extremely ill! The heat was becoming unbearable, and it was as if my body was on fire.

Then I had the strangest feeling. One that no-one would want to have. I was going to die. Then the feeling turned into a knowing. I was so scared, I even started to pray. The thought of contacting the dead was one thing, but joining them - no way!

With 2 small children to look after, surely it was not my time to die. I did not want to die. Not now. Not yet. Out of the blur of my impending demise, I saw my husband standing in front of me. I remember saying "I'm going to die".

Well, if you have ever seen someone in the midst of feeling very wretched, and indeed feeling very ill, you may have also heard them say they were about to die. You don't take it seriously, and he certainly didn't.

It was then that I felt a presence, and a feeling of great calm came over me. Something was happening that I did not as yet understand, but with a sense of knowing that this experience would somehow change my life, I let go of my fear completely.

I made my way back to bed, and somehow I managed to fall asleep. The next day I felt like someone who was split in two. I didn't quite know how to feel. Instead I tried to hold onto everything that was familiar and comforting. I turned to the memory of the presence that seemed to stand next to me, and I held onto the knowing that I had entered a cross-roads in my life.

However, I couldn't help feeling a little unsettled about what that meant. Where do you go when you need reassurance? You go to the place where you believe you will get help and answers, and that is exactly what I did. The following evening, Monday, I managed to drive myself to the Church. To this day, I don't know how I got there, but I did. Naively, I thought it would all be explained, but how wrong I was! No-one knew. They didn't have any answers. For the first time, I felt very alone.

What had begun as a search for the bridge between life and death, had taken on a different connotation altogether. I felt out of my depth, and I was frightened. Several days went by before I felt myself again. Time has a way of putting memories to rest, and that is what I did. What you don't understand, you put aside, believing that one day all will be revealed.

People live like that. What can't be explained either never happened or is camouflaged under the daily ritual of life. What you can't explain, you try to forget, and so I went back to the study of what others knew. Through their "expertise" and experience I gathered confidence to explore the art of clairvoyance through holding a personal item, such as jewellery or keys. My success rate was minimal in the beginning, but I soon learnt that success or failure was often through interpretation.

Spending hours practicing the art of "prophecy", as it was called, I began to develop an ability to predict the future, as well as having an insight into the past. It's amazing how many friends you suddenly have, all wanting to know what the future held for them. Of course, I obliged. Having such a skill, I felt needed and somewhat respected for what I was able to do.

My sense of ego grew, along with the number of new friends I had gathered to me. Those days were so busy, so full of social interaction, and of course, displaying my new found talent. My confidence grew as events occurred that I had predicted. I felt special then, believing that what I could do would help others make new choices, knowing the outcome of old ones.

However, life has a way of showing you what you don't want to see, and that is exactly what happened. A family crisis occurred that affected me greatly, and I desperately needed a friend. Family meant a great deal to me, and my heart was breaking for what they were going through.

Those whom I had helped so many times, went looking for someone else to fulfil their needs. It was a harsh lesson, but one I needed to learn. My inflated sense of worth was quickly given a dose of reality. After that, I viewed what I could do as a gift, rather than an opportunity to be popular.

Chapter 3

One day a friend invited me to accompany her to a metaphysical discussion group that met regularly. For a small donation, you could listen to a speaker share their insight and experiences, and you were also given lunch. When she told me that the topic was past lives, I wasn't really interested. I simply didn't believe that we lived more than one life, but reluctantly, I agreed to go. When we arrived, there were about 20 people crammed into the lounge room, and there were only a couple of seats left, albeit not together.

She headed down the other end of the room and I took the remaining seat near the door. Surrounded by people who obviously knew each other, I wasn't impressed, and wished she hadn't talked me into coming.

I noticed a young blonde woman enter the room. She'll be lucky, I thought to myself, all the seats are taken. Looking around the room, her gaze suddenly met mine. She stood there, staring at me, and I must admit, I was starting to feel quite uncomfortable. It was then that she walked over to me. "I feel I know you" she said. I shook my head and told her she was obviously mistaken. A strange look came over her face, and she said something that made me go cold. "I knew you in Egypt" she said. "That is where I knew you".

I have to say, in that moment I genuinely felt sorry for her. She was obviously one of those "crazies". I smiled and shook my head, because honestly I didn't quite know what to say.

It would be honest to say that I went to the meeting that day with a closed mind. Whilst I was open to ghosts and spirits, past lives were something that I had not given any thought to. I was taught that we lived one life, and had only one opportunity to get it right. After that, you had to work hard in the world beyond here to get to the ultimate place of awareness, which was in God's presence.

With that in mind, I listened to the speaker share his understanding of past lives. He was a man who appeared to be in his mid 50's, very articulate and who spoke at great length about the evidence that had been gathered of past lives. Whilst his talk was extremely interesting, I was still not convinced. A closed mind is hard to open, but when it does, it never closes again.

That day, my mind opened to the understanding that I had lived before. It happened when we were all asked to close our eyes, take a deep breath and allow ourselves to enter into a deep state of meditation. Within that deeper state of consciousness, we were to allow images of a past life to come to us. I did what I was asked, and quietly allowed myself to enter into meditation. Not expecting to see anything, I was very surprised to find myself transported into a large room that was being used for ceremonial purposes. An altar stood at the end of the room, with several people standing in front of it. One of them was holding a young baby that appeared to be the subject of a sacrifice. Horrified, I saw them murder the baby with what appeared to be a knife.

Then the scene quickly changed, and I found myself in a stone room with high ceilings. Light was coming in from a small opening high up, and a feeling of absolute grief engulfed me. It was then that I knew that the baby that had been sacrificed was, in fact, my baby. In shock, I opened my eyes, and tried to stifle the emotion that welled up inside me.

Looking over at the young blonde woman, I knew that she was somehow involved in what I had just experienced. In that moment, I knew I had been so very wrong. I had just experienced another life that held so much pain and sorrow.

My emotion overflowed, and all I could think of was to run, and that is what I did. I just got up and ran. Looking back now, that day opened up the doorway to a world that was to become so very important in my life in times to come. Needless to say, I felt extremely embarrassed to go back to that group, but one day I plucked up the courage and did so. Nothing was ever said, and in all the times that I went, I never saw that young woman there again.

Chapter 4

There can't be a story such as mine without including what is termed "a haunted house". The definition of such a place usually defies logic in some, and can be easily explained away by others. It all depends upon whether you are only open to what is within your range of "normal" or not. I had always been drawn to the classic haunting story, but to experience it was another thing, especially when the house was only several years old within a new housing estate.

My sister & her husband had moved to Queensland and bought a house in Collingwood Park, Ipswich, an outer suburb of Brisbane. One day she rang me, asking if I would spend a few days with her, as her husband would be away on a business trip and she felt a little nervous at the prospect of being left alone. At the time, I put in down to her being pregnant with her second child, and when she offered to pay half my airfare, I didn't need too much persuasion to say yes.

The timing was perfect. My husband was a school teacher, and as luck would have it, school holidays coincided with my trip to Queensland, and so we struck a deal. He would look after our 5 year old daughter until I got back, and I would take our 3 year old son with me.

Little did I realise then that my unexpected holiday in Queensland would prove to be a time that I would never, ever forget. I was about to embark upon a trip that would turn into a nightmare!

I had never been to her new home before, and so with great excitement, I boarded the plane to Brisbane. Looking after a 3 year old in the plane wasn't easy, but food and drink with a colouring book and pencils helped make the two hours pass fairly quickly. When we arrived at Brisbane airport, it was well into the afternoon. Too late to plan an outing, but it would be great to just catch up together.

Arriving in Brisbane, I felt eager to spend some relaxation time away from the routine of home. We arrived at her home in next to no time, and of course we didn't stop talking the entire way. I felt nothing unusual when I entered inside her house, and soon I was unpacked with time on my hands to spare!

After tea we put the children to bed and settled down for a relaxing evening together, but as the evening passed, I started to feel a little weary. It definitely was time to go to bed. I was to share with her, whilst her son was in his bed across the hall & my son was in the spare bedroom. Going to the bathroom to prepare for bed, I heard what sounded like footsteps on the gravel outside the window. I listened carefully, but I heard nothing more.

I dismissed it from my mind. Then I heard it again, and I began to feel a little apprehensive. My mind searched for an answer. Perhaps my sister had gone outside for something, and with that thought carefully in place, I felt somewhat relieved.

After finishing in the bathroom, I made my way to the bedroom, and found her sitting up in bed waiting for me. I just had to ask her, "Were you outside a few minutes ago?"

"No," she replied. "I have been waiting here for you. Why do you ask?"

"Because I heard footsteps on the gravel, just outside the window of the bathroom," I said. I remember the look she gave me, and it was one that I would see many times over the next few days. Her answer made me go cold.

"There is no gravel outside. There is only a garden bed."

I knew that I had heard footsteps in gravel. There was no mistaking that fact. However, I certainly wasn't about to go outside to solve the puzzle. I would do that in the morning. So, blissfully unaware of what was about to happen, I got into bed, ready for a good nights sleep. I had only just closed my eyes, when I heard it again. Footsteps on gravel. There was no mistaking it! I looked over to see if my sister was asleep. She wasn't.

"Did you hear that?" she asked. "Unfortunately, I did." I replied.

"I'm telling you, there isn't any gravel outside," she said, and I detected some alarm in her voice. In that moment, I just wished I was home again, safely tucked into my own bed.

We both lay there for quite some time, listening, but we heard nothing more. Time passed. I just couldn't keep my eyes open any longer, and I fell asleep. However, only a couple of hours had gone by when we were both woken by the bed moving and the bed covers being pulled off us.

Frozen with fear we just couldn't move, and the survival instinct of fight or flight was abandoned. I remember just laying there in complete bewilderment of what was happening.

Then something happened that cannot be explained, and has happened to me a number of times since. I fell asleep. In fact we both fell asleep, and the next thing I remember is waking up to the sun streaming through the windows. It was morning, and everything that had happened through the night seemed unreal, almost as if it was a dream.

There is something about a light sunny day that somehow has the ability to downplay the night-time jitters. What seemed so threatening last night disappeared under the promise of a perfect day. In fact, we laughed at it, describing ourselves as being silly females with an over inflated sense of imagination. We both didn't believe that for a moment, but it seemed to fit nicely into our denial. After all, the day lay ahead and the weather was glorious.

After spending a great day shopping and relaxing, night time came around once again, and a sense of trepidation welled up inside of me. Going to bed that night, we were both feeling quite uneasy, and we weren't feeling so brave anymore. Closing my eyes, I prayed that the morning light would come quickly. No such luck! It wasn't long before it became very obvious that something was there!

My sister was also awake, and she whispered, "Do you feel something?"

"Yes," I replied. "I do."

We both lay there in the darkness that night, wishing that we were anywhere but there. How I longed for my own bed, that seemed in that moment so far away. The feeling in the room was one of foreboding, that something was terribly wrong. Thankfully, there were no more footsteps, but instead there was this terrible presence that seemed to close in on us.

The light from the lamp seemed our only option. At least it took away the darkness of the room. We both slept fitfully that night, determined to find someone who could help us get rid of whatever it was. In the morning we looked in the local papers to see if we could find someone who could send whatever it was on it's way. We found the name of a woman who advertised herself as a spirit medium.

Picking up the phone, we rang her straight away, and after explaining what was happening, she offered to come and see us later that afternoon. What a relief! Whatever it was, we didn't want it!

I was extremely naive in those days. It was very early in my journey and I was too ready to listen to anyone else who had the answers to everything I was still too scared to experience.

We went to the sanctuary of the shops that day, feeling safe amongst the hordes of tourists and people who were enjoying the day. They were the lucky ones I thought. I bet they don't have a menacing ghost ready and willing to frighten them out of their wits in the middle of the night!

They certainly didn't look half asleep like us. My heart sank at the thought of returning to the house.

The time came when we had to return to the house, and so we reluctantly made our way back. We decided to put the children down for a sleep, so we could tell our story to this woman without any interruptions. I felt anxious as I waited for her to arrive, and I wondered what she would find. What if she found nothing at all, and then it came back later that night? It's amazing how many thoughts go round in your mind at a time like that.

A short time later there was a knock on the door, and there stood our 'guardian angel' all dressed in white, ready to save the day! Or so we hoped. She stepped into the house and introduced herself. Whilst we went into detail about everything that had happened, she listened intently.

Then, looking straight at me, she said, "You need to get that jumper off immediately and put on something that is much lighter in colour. You shouldn't be wearing black, it's a negative colour."

I quickly ran off to the bedroom to find the lightest coloured jumper I could find, and in doing so I threw my black jumper to the floor. I can laugh at it now, but I didn't wear that jumper for ages after.

Walking down the hallway towards the main bedroom where we had been sleeping, she stopped to look at a macrame owl that was hanging on the wall, just outside the bedroom. She seemed horrified by what she felt from it, telling us it held negative energy, and it had to go! So it was taken off the wall and put straight into the garage.

Her next point of call was the bedroom, where she decidedly looked uncomfortable. We stood in the doorway, afraid to venture in, not quite knowing what to do.

What she said next sent a chill up my spine. "There is an evil spirit here".

Well, as you can imagine, we just freaked! That's when you want to run to the nearest church and ask for a room.

It's amazing she didn't have an antidote or even an explanation about what she had found. Instead, she just gave us a cross to put on the wall of the bedroom, telling us to pray for protection when we went to bed.

She then went to a cupboard in the hallway where my sister kept some books she had collected on the paranormal, and after inspecting them, she insisted that there were several that also held negative energies, and they had to go too!

With that, she said goodbye and was out of the door. So much for the rescue party! Oh, I forget to mention, it cost us heaps! They don't come cheap those people. Makes you wonder if she has a supplier of crosses at a wholesale price.

After she had gone my sister took the macrame owl to the incinerator. Putting her beloved books and the macrame owl, along with some other rubbish she had collected, she lit a match. That was that, or so we thought. We decided to go out again to get some tea. Of course, it was an excuse to take a break from the house. Returning back a couple of hours later, we were in for a shock.

You may not believe this, but it is true .. on the floor of the kitchen was a section of the macrame owl, about the size of the palm of your hand, with it's edges burnt. We just couldn't believe our eyes! This was just terrible! What was going on? We went through every possibility we could to try and find a logical answer, but we could find none. None at all. To this day, it remains a mystery.

That night we slept under the cross that we hung on the wall above the bed, and we both contributed to a long heartfelt prayer that we hoped would work. Unfortunately, it didn't. Just as the night before, we both felt a sinister presence. Enough was enough!

We both decided then and there that we were going back to my place in Melbourne the next day. She would wait for her husband to return home before she came back. There was no way we were going to spend another night in this room! So we went into the bedroom across the hall where her young son slept.

Well, he certainly looked peaceful, so we would just have to squeeze in with him. Feeling somewhat relieved, as well as feeling very cramped in that bed, we tried to get some sleep. However, that wasn't to be, for whatever it was had followed us to her son's room.

She had a large portable electric heater that she hadn't used for quite some time, and it was sitting in the corner of the room. It suddenly started to make loud banging sounds, similar to when a heater cools down. This went on for quite some time, and we both lay there frozen with fear.

The first light of morning brought the greatest relief to both of us. Her son seemed unperturbed by it all and had slept throughout the night, but we had not.

The next morning we made plans to leave as soon as we could get a flight. Luckily, we were able to get on a late morning flight to Melbourne, and so two very tired women and two very awake and active children boarded a flight to safety.

In concluding this story, the problems continued when she returned to her home with her husband. Not to the extent that we had experienced them, but there were times when it was obvious that something was there, that certainly wasn't friendly.

She shared the story with one of her neighbours who told her that the housing estate was built close to where they used to mine for coal. Perhaps the footsteps in gravel were footsteps in shoal.

This all happened at the point of my development when my psychic abilities were only beginning to emerge, and whatever was within the house had somehow reacted to my energy, combined with my sisters. At that point in my development, it was far beyond my capabilities to combat

I couldn't understand what it was or where it had come from. However, when we got back to Melbourne, my sister confessed to using the Ouija board a few weeks earlier with her next door neighbour. Who knows what they attracted.

I was so glad to be home.

Chapter 5

As time went by my confidence in my ability to interact with those who reside in the spiritual worlds grew. I was becoming very proficient at psychic readings and suddenly I found myself in the middle of so many opportunities to test out my psychic abilities. My list of friends grew and grew – funny about that!

It was in 1984 when I was encouraged by my friends to start a psychic development group. I was a little reluctant at first, wondering if I had the abilities needed to do so, but I was soon persuaded to give it a go, which I did. It wasn't a large group, just myself and five other ladies, meeting once a week at my home. The group ran for 2 years, finishing in 1986. It was a wonderful experience, and we certainly had our share of unexplained experiences during that time.

When you are on a journey of discovery, you have to learn to eat "humble pie". All you believed in that had previously been the staple diet of your life, has to experience a metamorphosis. Growth means change, and you have to be prepared to let so much go that has been so meaningful and precious in your life, in order for something else to take it's place. If you can do that, then you have embarked upon a journey that will take you to places that you would never have dreamed existed.

Such was the case when I was invited to join a "physical phenomenon group".

In the mid 1800's the Fox sisters, Maggie and Kate, alleged that they communicated with spirits through a code, which involved a series of raps in answer to their questions. This was the first physical demonstration of communication between this world and the next. From their experiences, Spiritualism was born. By the early 1900's there were many mediums who were supposedly communicating with the Spirit realm, and physical phenomenon groups were extremely popular.

When I was asked to join such a group, I was beside myself. I hardly knew the people involved, and when I asked them why they had asked me, they replied that they had been instructed to do so by the Spirit realm. Who was I to question that? Another powerful chapter in my journey of discovery was about to begin.

The group met in a small downstairs room in a suburban home. The windows were completely covered by heavy duty curtains that were specially designed to block out all light. At the other end of the room was an inbuilt wardrobe with double sliding doors. One side of the wardrobe was shelves, and the other side was the hanging space for clothes. It is imperative that my description is accurate, as the wardrobe had an important part to play in what happened there.

Six chairs were placed around the room, and in the centre was a small table. We were each given a small badge to wear, painted with iridescent paint that allowed it to glow in the dark. The iridescent paint was also on the surrounds of the wardrobe doors and around the outside of the small table.

It was explained to me that natural light or light from an electric light bulb interfered with the energy needed for communication, and the iridescent paint would allow us to see any activity that may eventuate in the room. As well as that, our badges would show where we were at all times, therefore eliminating any doubt of someone cheating.

The room was carpeted and we were instructed to take our shoes off. This would allow us to feel any vibration or movement in the floor. It would also eliminate any noise that heavy shoes may make if they inadvertently made contact with the legs of the table or chairs.

Each person was given a glass of water which was placed in front of them on the table. With all of that in place, my first experience in a physical phenomenon group began. This was so totally new to me. No-one I knew had ever been involved in such a group, and I was honoured to be asked, to say the least. Excitement and nervousness went hand in hand as the light was turned off, and we were ready to begin. The room was extremely dark, with only the light from the iridescent paint outlining the doors of the cupboard and the edges of the table, not forgetting our badges, showing where each person was seated.

If you think we sat in silence, then you're wrong. They had earlier explained to me that they used nostalgia through songs to attract those from the Spirit world. Therefore, they had put together a number of songs that would provoke a strong response. Songs from the war years of the 1940's were chosen, along with ballads from the 50's and 60's.

Thank goodness I knew a lot of the words to the older songs, due to my parent's sing-a-longs with their friends at parties.

Everything I had learnt was discarded. Quiet meditation music with candles was a thing of the past. Now I was sitting in a dark room with a group of people singing old war songs and ballads. I could have been forgiven for thinking "what am I doing here?"

However, I did not, and sang along with the rest, waiting for the very loud raps they spoke of to eventuate. We didn't have long to wait, and the Spirit world, if that was who it was, put on an amazing performance.

Loud knocks on walls were one thing, but I also felt them under my feet and under the seat of my chair. Logic could not explain what was happening. No- one moved on their seats as the raps became extremely loud, moving around the room very, very quickly. Certain songs evoked a greater response, whilst through other songs, nothing was heard. I was truly amazed by what was happening, and as the evening drew to a close, I said a quiet thank you for the opportunity to experience such an event.

The light was switched on, and our eyes gradually began to adjust to the bright light. Everyone sat quietly, as if their thoughts were not as yet in this world. We then made out way out to the kitchen for a well earned cup of coffee.

Over the next few weeks it was decided to attempt to generate a greater physical manifestation by using methods used by Spiritualist mediums in the early 1900's, whereby a medium sat on a chair in a cupboard, with a heavy curtain hanging over the front. This allowed for an extremely dark and secluded place in which to be. The medium then entered a deep level of consciousness, or trance state, in order to be a generator for spirit manifestation.

With this in mind, one of the group was chosen for his wonderful 'mediumistic' abilities to be the one to sit in the cupboard. The memory of what happened in that room during the next few months will stay with me forever. I have only shared it with a select few, but it is now time to tell the story to all who read this book. There are several specific experiences that happened, alongside the raps and physical sensations that were felt during our sessions. These experiences will stretch your boundary of belief, as they did mine, but I assure you they really happened.

One evening, as we were singing along with the music, one of the group started sneezing. She apologised and continued on. When the lights were put back on, there was a tissue placed in front of each person on the small table. After some discussion about this manifestation, it was remembered that there were a few tissues left in a box on the top shelf of the cupboard.

Now, because there was someone sitting in the cupboard throughout the entire session, on the side where clothes would normally be hung, the sliding door was pushed across towards the other side of the cupboard, where the shelves were. Therefore, two doors covered the shelves where the tissues were kept. Upon sliding the two doors across to the other side, the tissue box was found to be empty.

It could be explained by someone placing the tissues there during the session, but at no time did anyone move, except to take a drink of water from their glass on the table, and it was not possible for anyone to reach across the table, placing tissues in front of each person, without getting up from their chair. It was decided that the Spirit world had a great sense of humour.

Weeks went by without anything significant happening, until one night when we were all deeply into our repertoire of songs, one of the group cried out that something had dropped onto their head. The music was quickly turned down and we all heard multiple sounds of something falling from above onto the table. We were quickly instructed to keep very still and to not move, which we did. Nothing else happened that night, and we all couldn't wait until the session was finished and the light switched on, to reveal what had happened.

As the light came on, we all looked on the table to see what it was. However, there was nothing there. It was then that someone noticed that in between their feet was a 50 cent coin. I looked down to the floor, and there in between my own feet was a 20 cent and 50 cent coin, placed perfectly together.

All in all, there was a total of 6 coins, some of which were 50 cent pieces and others were 20 cent pieces. They had been placed carefully by something unknown at the feet of several of the group. All in all, there was one coin for each of us.

To have coins fall from above onto the table was one thing. However, to have them placed between our feet was another. It was impossible for anyone in that room that night to have been involved in such a feat.

As you are reading this, you are no doubt shaking your head in disbelief, and I would understand that you would do so. However, each person wore a badge that shone in the dark that night, and the medium in the cupboard, who was a big man, would have easily been detected if he had moved.

We all took our coin home with us, and I carefully wrapped mine in a tissue and placed it in my bedside drawer. However, within a week it had disappeared.

The group used various members to "try out" in the cupboard, sometimes with success, and sometimes the night was very quiet. It was during one of the nights when no-one was in there that upon turning the light back on, we discovered the curtain to the cupboard had been tied in a double knot that was so tight, it could only be undone by using a screwdriver to loosen it.

On another occasion, the wire that was used to hang the curtain was completely stretched to such a degree that part of the curtain was on the floor. All of these events were powerful evidence that something was intersecting with the physical world and making its presence known.

It is at this point that I need to share one of the most powerful experiences we had. On that particular night the laws of physics were completed overturned. It was during one of the evenings when no-one was seated in the cupboard. On this particular night activity in the room had been constant, with extremely loud bangs and knocks repeatedly being heard.

What I am going to tell you next sounds totally unbelievable, yet it happened! The curtain had been removed from the cupboard and the two doors were closed. Remembering that the outline of the doors could be seen because of the iridescent paint. We had often seen shadows move across these doors during our sessions, and the paint allowed us to acknowledge when this happened.

It was about halfway through the night when one of the doors stared to move backwards and forwards to the music. As the music began to quicken, the door also moved more quickly. If this wasn't enough, it actually lifted out of its bottom runner and, at an angle, moved backwards and forwards many, many times to the music. I remember thinking "no-one, just no-one would believe what I am seeing".

The man who was conducting the group, and whose home we were in, got scared, very scared. He quickly finished the session and put the light on. There, in front of our eyes, was the door, just hanging there, out of its runner.

It was impossible for it to have come out of its sliding runner by itself, and to have moved in such a way to the music, well, something very powerful was behind it all, and certainly having a game with us!

On another occasion, we were all sitting in the room, listening and waiting for some activity, when the table began to levitate. Remembering that the outer edges of the table were easily seen because of the iridescent paint. It lifted about 30 cm from the floor, shaking a little and sending the glasses of water spilling everywhere. However, one glass filled with water lasted the distance, and stayed upright. Nearly everyone got wet. It was amazing to see and experience, but that was the first and only time that it happened.

One other event took place that was a little different than those I have mentioned, but I feel it is worth speaking about. After the conclusion of one of our evenings, one of the "sitters" complained that her wedding ring had gone out of shape. Instead of being round, it was now oval.

A short time after, she found her husband and another woman together. She filed for divorce.

After about 14 months I felt that I had experienced and learnt what I needed to. It had been an amazing experience, and one I would never forget, but it was time to move on, and so I did. I left the group and prepared myself for the next chapter on my journey of discovery. If you stay in one place too long, then it's no longer a journey.

Chapter 6

Just when you least expect, your life takes you in a completely different direction. This happened to me when I answered the telephone one evening and the woman on the other end said, "You don't know me, but I was given your telephone number by a mutual friend".

It turned out that she, along with three others, ran an organisation called The Mind Research, which met monthly. Her job was to find different speakers to address their members at each meeting, and would I be interested in being one of their speakers?

I have to admit, I took a big deep breath before I answered. It was a great opportunity, but I suddenly had this yucky feeling deep inside my stomach. It's fear of course, but then why listen to fear?

"Oh yes, I would love to," I heard myself saying. All the while, I was thinking to myself, "What the hell am I going to talk about?"

She told me to send her a small description of the talk, which she would circulate to all the members.

Putting the phone down, I wondered what had I let myself in for? From the brave to the brave-less! Now I had to come up with something that would keep them all interested for 3 1/2 hours – with a break in-between, of course! No mean feat, but then it was a journey of discovery after all. What was the worst that could happen? I didn't even want to think about it.

The only experience I had had was speaking to small groups of people, and most of them I had come to know quite well. This was completely different, but then I was never one to not have a go at anything.

Over the next few days I contemplated my fate. I would be speaking to people who had listened to so many lecturers, about so many different subjects. Now, what was I going to speak about that they hadn't heard before? That question went over and over in my mind. The answer finally came to me. I would speak about my own personal experiences – now, that was new!

The day finally arrived and with my sister and a friend in toe, we set off for my debut. I have to say at this point that I had no notes at all. What I had experienced couldn't be written down, it had to come from my heart.

When we got there, I was warmly greeted by the organisers of the event, who led me into the main hall. Oh, my goodness! There were about 150 chairs in the hall, and they were quickly being taken. This was no small group. This was big! My stomach turned upside down. There was no turning back. This was it.

Now, take a moment to imagine this scene. Here I was, in front of an audience of about 150 people, who have all paid to listen to me, yes, little old me. I have no notes, nothing! All I had was what was near and dear to me, and that was the story of my journey and my experiences.

The difference between success and disaster lay in my ability to not freeze and lose track of what had been so profound and important to me in my life so far.

If I could do that, then I would be able to share who I had been and who I had become. After my introduction, I took a deep breath and spoke from my heart. That day was one of the most memorable days in my life. I not only spoke to the people there, but I spoke to myself.

As I did so, I realised how much I had changed. From the insecure and sometimes brash person to the insightful and progressive person I was becoming.

All my memories came flashing back to me, from the difficult and frustrating times to the funny and ridiculous. They had all contributed to the person that I had become. The journey of discovery is a long one, and when I reach the end of my time here, I believe there will still be so much more that I just didn't have time to uncover.

That is what it is all about. It is not about knowing. It is about discovering. I had the best time that day, and they must have too, for I was asked to come back again. Now, you can't ask for better than that!

On one of my return trips I spoke about something that had been on my mind for quite some time. I wanted to conduct a weekend workshop, but for a price that was affordable to everyone.

There were many people at that time conducting workshops that were so extremely expensive, that I decided to bring out that radical part of me and create an once-off opportunity for people to come to a Weekend Workshop for what it cost to run it. I would not receive any profit at all. Only my costs would be covered. Somehow I wanted to give these people something, as much as I wanted to give something to myself.

The place that I chose accommodated over 50 people. It had a main lecture room where I could run the workshop, and a dining room where meals were served. All this was situated on acres of beautiful rolling green hills with giant gum trees. It was just magic. It was a huge success, and I took away from that weekend so many wonderful memories that I still treasure today. That weekend was the first of many that I ran over the next few years.

Then something happened that changed the course of my life once more. I was taking a well earned break, just before going to dinner, on the first day of a Weekend Workshop, when something happened to me.

At this point I need to say that I had felt a little restless during the day, and didn't feel myself. It wasn't that I was unwell, I just felt restless and a little flat. Something was obviously wrong, for I normally felt on a high during the entire weekend, and this wasn't like me.

I remember what happened next, as if it was yesterday. I was in my room when an incredible wave of claustrophobia came over me. In that moment I knew, I absolutely knew, I was asleep somewhere, and I was dreaming all of this. I looked at the two other people in the room and knew they weren't real, they were illusion.

Everything came in on me, and I felt trapped in my body and in my room. I remember screaming inside my mind, "I want to wake up, I just want to wake up out of this dream".

It was the most frightening experience of my life.

I decided to go outside and take in some fresh air. I stood for ages looking up at the stars, but even they seemed too close. I just felt so trapped. It's not easy when you have such a powerful experience that shakes you to your core, and know that you have to pull yourself together, for there is still one day to go, and you just can't lose it! You have an obligation to 50 other people. What you can't explain to yourself, you surely can't explain it to them.

Pulling myself together, I went into the Dining Room and joined the others. Thankfully, the claustrophobic feeling began to diminish, and the rest of the Weekend passed without incident. However, my experience had created an emotional imbalance within me, and the next few days and weeks were difficult indeed.

Whatever had happened to me had shifted my whole perception of what was real and meaningful to me. The memory of those powerful images didn't leave me, and I found myself pondering upon what was indeed real and meaningful in my life. Nothing was ever the same after that.

What had been important to me had been wiped away in an instant. My world and my life turned upside down. I felt totally alone in a world that I feared I could no longer believe in. This feeling was like a heavy cloud over me as I struggled to maintain a relativity point to myself and life in the next few weeks.

My life seemed to be only illusion. I asked myself, "What was the purpose to it, if it was only illusion? Everything that I had put into my life, was it all for nothing?" These were the questions that I asked myself. Which direction was I to take, when I couldn't see anything clearly.

Little did I know then that I was soon to have another experience that would influence my life even more than what had just happened.

It was in November, 1991, just a few weeks after my experience when I had an experience through the night. I found myself standing in front of three robed figures within a large room. One stepped forward and with his hand outstretched, gestured to the wall behind him. It immediately disappeared, and in its place was a scene whereby Planet Earth was shown in a starry night sky.

"It needs light," he said

I don't know what came over me, for I replied, "Surely that is your job."

He looked at me and shook his head. At that moment, I just knew that I shouldn't have said that! "That is the trouble," he said, "you just don't believe enough."

When I awoke, the memory of his words kept repeating themselves over and over again in my mind. Especially "That is the trouble, you just don't believe enough. You have to change quickly and drastically".

I wondered what he meant. What was it about myself that had to change "quickly and drastically", and what was meant by "You just don't believe enough"? I had plenty of beliefs, which one did he mean?

I look back at that time in my life and I smile. I realise now that I was so full of beliefs that I had not left room for the belief in my own power of light.

He certainly did not mean that I, alone, could personally light up Planet Earth! He meant that we all have within us that light that we need to experience, so that we can create change within ourselves.

Whilst we look outward to a higher power to solve our personal problems and the problems that we, collectively, as humanity, have created upon this planet of ours, we will never be aware of the light that we have within our inner selves.

My perspective of reality had definitely shifted, but all in all, I was a different person because of it.

I knew had reached the end of a chapter of my life, and I was eager to start the next one.

They say there is a fine line separating illusion from reality. I have often wondered about that line. An invisible point where fact and fiction are separated. The actual point where that line is, has been contested throughout history itself. In fact, wars have been fought and many have died because of it. In the end, it all comes down to belief. Whether it is illusion or reality is decided totally by belief. However, the question is – where did belief originate from in the first place?

Another word for belief is 'faith'. Haven't we all heard that one so many times? Have 'faith', which also means – have 'belief' is often used when there are no answers to the questions we have. So, instead of answers, we have 'faith' or 'belief'. In summary, the invisible point that separates illusion from reality is determined by 'no answers'.

Makes sense, doesn't it?

The only way to find answers is to look for them yourself, but you will never find answers if you are afraid of what you will find. You have to be ready to experience what you may never have believed in. In doing so, your perception of yourself and the world around you may change dramatically. If you are not willing to do this, then leave it alone! Just accept that there may never be answers to the questions you have.

However, for those who have the courage and conviction to find answers, then do it! Never look back at the person you use to be. Just look ahead with the knowing that you are on a journey of awakening, that will take you to the next discovery, and so on. Never stop! Not ever! The road to remembering is littered with those who never had the courage to keep going, and they will try to stop you.

Whatever you do, don't listen to them! Their need to hold onto the person they believed themselves to be, was greater than their desire to find the truth. That is what this book is all about. It's the true story of my life, and my quest for the answers that no-one wanted me to know. With all that said .. I'll continue the story.

It was early 1993 when something happened, whereby I was forced to reconsider whether I would continue with my quest for answers. It was when my children were threatened by something that did not want me to continue.

When I made the decision to write this story, I made a pledge that I would tell it as it happened. What seems so frightening at first can often be seen totally different a little later, but in this case, it was years later.

What happened, that seemed so horrific at first, became the greatest clue to the most powerful answer of all. Without this experience, the rest of the story could not have taken place.

It all started with my son, who was 15 at the time. His bedroom was on the upper level of the house, next to my daughter's room. My bedroom was on the next level down. One morning he came down to breakfast looking absolutely terrible. When I asked him if he was alright, he told me a story that sent a shiver down my spine...

He had a vivid experience in the night, which he assured me was not a dream! He was standing in front of a large black energy mass that was seated in an ornate chair. As he looked at it, he felt completely swamped by a powerful sense of fear and intimidation. It stood up and he heard words coming from it.

"Tell your Mother to stop! If she doesn't, she will die!" He said he felt terrified. The only other description he could give me was it had red eyes.

If that was the only experience he had, it could have been put down to an active imagination, coupled with a subconscious desire for me to not be involved in my investigation into the paranormal.

However, that was not the case, for that very night, he had another experience. This time this large energy mass spoke to him about failing to influence me to stop what I was doing. It told him that if he didn't help it, then it would go to his sister and make her enforce it's will upon her.

He was totally terrified!

When he told me, we decided to not involve my daughter, who was 17 at the time, for there was no need to instil fear in her because of his bizarre experience.

That night there was a knock on my bedroom door, and my daughter came in, sounding absolutely 'freaked out'. She spoke to me quietly, not wanting to wake her father.

"Can I bring my mattress down here with you, because I have just had this most horrible experience?" After asking her what happened, she told me that a large black energy mass came to her and told her that she had to get me to stop doing what I was doing. Knowing that my son hadn't told her about his experiences, I knew then that this was a very serious situation.

Naturally, I agreed for her to bring her mattress down to my room and sleep. However, it didn't stop there. For whatever happened upstairs in her room, continued in mine. She laid down on her mattress, which she had placed on the floor next to me, and tried to sleep. I laid awake for a little while, but soon went to sleep.

It was only in the morning that I found out that her experience had continued. She told me that she had trouble sleeping. The next thing she knows is that a large dark figure, which was different that the one she had seen in her room, loomed over her. Her fear increased when she found she couldn't move.

She then noticed that a very small elf-like being that seemed to emanate light was sitting on the bookcase behind the dark figure, just swinging it's legs.

At that point, the dark figure seemed unaware of it, but when it did realise what was there, it became very afraid, and instantly disappeared. She recollects watching this elf-figure for some time before drifting off to sleep.

Sometime in the night, she woke up, and to her amazement, this elf-like figure was still there! When she woke up in the morning, it was gone. After that experience, there were no more visitations of that energy to either my son or my daughter. Needless to say, I didn't stop!

Chapter 7

Transition is never easy from one chapter of life to another. Whilst I had changed, many did not choose to view it as beneficial to them. They did not understand what had happened to me, nor did they even want to.

The Workshops that I had conducted for many years began to wind down, and I considered conserving my energy for more personal work with just a few people, and that is exactly what I did ...

In loving memory ...

Diane, you leave us with what you had most of, and that is truly love.

This message to you, the reader, was given during the final review before publishing:

"A Life Worth Living" is a message about remembering we all have a part to play in our *own* remembering of why we are here. What purpose do you have? Is it to cycle around forever on the same pathway of understanding nothing, waiting for life itself to provide all the answers?

It never will. I began this journey because of something that happened to me many years ago and it changed my life forever. It could change yours, if you let it.

For those who are wanting to know the answers, start searching. For those who are not wanting to know, go back to your lives. But for those who do want to know, go inward. For only there will you find the truth of your awakening to a greater part of yourself that can give to you the knowing of where to go from here.

We all have a purpose. Some within life and some beyond. But in the end, we are all a part of a greater mission that leads us all home. And that is where we all need to be. Wake up to what you are, for goodness sake! And come home. It is time.

No longer do you need to hide in the shadows for fear of remembering that which you cannot obtain. All is available. All is ready. The door is open and we are waiting for you. You just need to remember. That is all.

We welcome you.

Afterword

... The final words in this book were written before Diane had a chance to tell the rest of her story. It is now 2023, and I wish to attempt to bridge the gap between then and now as some form of closure. At the very least, some form of explanation to help you, the reader, to understand what happened next.

Diane passed away in 2020. She called her life "A Life Worth Living", and it was. If you believe in something greater, if you believe you are here for a reason that goes beyond the illusion of this life, then you all owe it to yourself to find out what that is and live your own 'Life Worth Living'.

I do not known exactly when Diane wrote the beginning of this last chapter. Diane was always writing, always investigating, always seeking out new ways to dig deeper and get to the answers.

'A Life Worth Living' does not yet touch upon one of the most powerful and influential parts of Diane's life - the energy of Elonias. I would direct you to the accompanying book "The Journey Home with Elonias'. This is a compilation of works given through Diane's mediumship up to 1992. Elonias is the Light of what is Real. A representative of light from beyond the illusion of reality. Diane's journey and story of the emergence of Elonias into her life is profound, breaking away images and illusions for what is Real to emerge.

The beginning of the 7th chapter of this book is profoundly connected to the mission that became Diane's life. She did not complete the end of this book as she intended, but she did complete the end of her story. Diane achieved something in her life and death that makes it possible for us all to go 'Home'. That is a fact.

True to her word, Diane entered into a period of many years of personal investigation and research work. Diane and I were married in 2003. I had the privilege and destiny of joining her in the single most important journey of all - to remember 'what' one is, and why one is here. Our work together delved into the deepest reaches of space and time, and the farthest dimensions beyond the boundaries of belief.

Diane followed the directive of Elonias to the very end... and beyond. I had the privilege of being with my wife in the moment she passed away... when she went home. It was a moment prophesied almost 20 years earlier. One can never truly predict the meaning of prophecy at the time it is given. Perhaps it is just as well. However, therein is the humility, wonder and profundity of a Greater Plan that works in cryptic ways, and always with love at its centre. There is a humility in this. Without humility and awareness, one has nothing.

During the precious and timeless years of working, living and loving with Diane, Beings of Light by the names of Mikael, Amoen and others continued to guide us along our path. At times our path was extremely difficult and very isolated, but always true and Real. To be in communication with the Light of all that is 'Real' is nothing less than the greatest privilege of my life, and I believe any life.

Diane completed her mission, and she sacrificed everything she knew for a greater cause. Diane lived as she died, in servitude and devotion to love and to what is Real.

The 'New Program' of light was activated in this timeline of our reality in 2020. It is not easy to connect the first stage of Diane's journey and life with her final stages... she simply travelled so very far.

To this end, the 'Shift' that occurred at the point of Diane's passing was a result of over 43 years of research and investigation into the nature of this reality, why we are here and an awakening and openness to the beauty of the Real that has entered this illusion to take us home.

Diane's and my life was a constant investigative experience of mediumship and communication, constant research and continuous questioning and searching, mind time-travel, out-of-body experiences, inter-dimensional contact, spiritual and aetheric journeys, in-depth research about formulas of light and the Greater Plan of creation itself, the mind, star systems, light coding, energy and so much more... there was no end, and it continues today in her name. So many were lost here long ago, and so many have now been found.

There is far more of this story still to tell, and I intend to somehow put to paper 'Our Life Worth Living', all about the life experiences Diane and I had together since we met in 1993.

I hope you have enjoyed reading Diane's "A Life Worth Living'. No one is more heartfelt than I when I say I wish Diane had the chance to finish her book...

Diane was and is an extraordinary woman. Whilst we are all 'One', and whilst Elonias reminds us "I am that what you are also", I have to say Diane was a one of a kind.

We should all be 'one of a kind' in our own lives. Be the sound of that 'what' you are at all times.

Keep loving, always. Not the image of love, but Real love. To understand the depth of what this statement means, I encourage you to read the works of Elonias as compiled by Diane in the book, 'The Journey Home'.

Remember always you are more than who you believe yourself to be. Journey beyond boundaries of belief. Don't ever stop. Listen inwardly. Wake up.

In all humility, on behalf of Diane, I leave you with what I have most of, and that is truly love.

... Jason

Available Reading:

The Journey Home with Elonias
Diane Swaffield

The Greatest Story Never Told
Amoen, Diane Swaffield

The Temple of Remembrance
Diane Swaffield

Upon the Sands of Time
Diane Swaffield

Available Viewing:

'The Illusion of Reality' Documentary
Written, produced & Narrated by Jason Swaffield

Online Resources:

eloniasfoundation.com
thetimecentre.com

www.ingramcontent.com/pod-product-compliance
Lightning Source LLC
Chambersburg PA
CBHW071035080526
44587CB00015B/2630